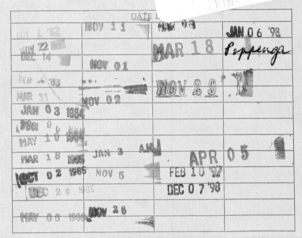

WHY MOUNT ST. HELENS BLEW ITS TOP

**by Kathryn Allen Goldner
and Carole Garbuny Vogel**

Illustrations by Roberta Aggarwal

DILLON PRESS, INC.   MINNEAPOLIS, MINNESOTA

For Mark, David, and Dotty

551.2
GoL

13550

Library of Congress Cataloging in Publication Data

Goldner, Kathryn Allen.
  Why Mount St. Helens blew its top.

  Bibliography: p. 83
  Includes index.
  SUMMARY: Describes the events leading up to the
May 18, 1980, eruption of Mount St. Helens and the
destruction that resulted. Also discusses the general
characteristics of volcanoes, why and when they occur,
how eruptions can be predicted, and some famous
eruptions throughout history.
  1. Saint Helens, Mount (Wash.)—Eruption, 1980—
Juvenile Literature.
  [1. Saint Helens, Mount (Wash.)—Eruption, 1980. 2.
Volcanoes] I. Vogel, Carole Garbuny. II. Title.
  QE523.S23G64   551.2'1   81-12482

  ISBN 0-87518-219-4   AACR2

Dillon Press, Inc., 500 South Third Street
Minneapolis, Minnesota 55415

Printed in the United States of America

Mount St. Helens

On May 18, 1980, Mount St. Helens erupted in an incredible display of volcanic force. It claimed at least sixty lives, killed millions of fish, knocked down trees for miles, set thousands of acres on fire, destroyed Spirit Lake, altered the course of the Toutle River, stopped shipping on the Columbia River, and changed the lives of many communities in the Pacific Northwest.

The story begins with the dramatic events on the day of the May 18 eruption. Some of the people who were killed chose to risk their lives: Harry Truman, the eighty-three-year-old lodge owner who lived by Spirit Lake; and David Johnston, the brave young scientist who climbed the slopes of the active volcano. After the eruption, nearby cities and towns struggled to cope with a blizzard of ash that made travel dangerous. In the years to come, more serious problems may be caused by the mountain of mud which roared down the rivers that drain the mountain.

Why did Mount St. Helens blow its top? A brief look at the science of volcanoes explains why and where they occur. People have lived in the shadow of active volcanoes for thousands of years. The stories of famous eruptions—Krakatoa, Mount Vesuvius, Mont Pelée—are told from the point of view of the people who lived near them. Are any of the other Cascade volcanoes about to erupt? A look at the history of Mount St. Helens and some other high Cascade peaks hints at some startling possibilities. It also explores answers to the question: Is Mount St. Helens going to blow its top again?

Illustrations

Acknowledgments

We would like to thank the following people for their assistance in putting together this book: Special thanks go to Dotty Burstein for her invaluable criticisms and encouragement, and to Bill Lokey of the Washington State Department of Emergency Services for answering technical questions and helping to locate photographs; thanks also go to David Roberts, Don Bockler, Leona Martin, Karen Gabler, and Carol deGrave for their suggestions, our husbands Mark Vogel and David Goldner for their encouragement, and to our editor Tom Schneider for his help.

Contents

1 A Volcano Blows Its Top

Snow and ice covered the top of Mount St. Helens. The sparkling waters of Spirit Lake nestled at its base. Trees and flowers grew on its slopes. Deer and elk grazed in the forest and meadows. Birds sang. Tumbling streams crisscrossed the mountain. The streams formed rivers that flowed to the Pacific Ocean. People hiked the mountain and enjoyed its peaceful wilderness.

On May 18, 1980, the sun rose into a cloudless sky. The forest was unusually quiet. No wind stirred the leaves. The squirrels did not chatter, and the birds did not sing. Suddenly, the stillness was shattered; two huge earthquakes shook the

mountain. Solid earth crumbled and gave way. A landslide plunged down the mountainside. Long cracks appeared in the ground.

Then it happened! Hot gases trapped inside Mount St. Helens exploded violently. The entire north side of the mountain blew apart!

Hot ash, rock, and dirt shot twelve miles high and formed a dark cloud that filled the sky. Day seemed to turn into night. Rocks and heavy clumps of mud rained down on the forest below. A blizzard of ash fell from the sky.

Ash fell on the slopes of Mount St. Helens. In places it was as much as six feet deep. People and animals were buried. The ash looked like fine gray sand, but it had the odor of cement powder. Winds carried the gritty powder away from the volcano. It fell on trees and flowers. It fell on cars and bridges. There was enough ash to cover much of the state of Washington east of Mount St. Helens. A dusting even fell on Denver, Colorado, a thousand miles away.

This violent explosion proved that Mount St. Helens was no ordinary mountain. It was a sleeping volcano that had just awakened.

The eruption created a powerful shock wave. In less than one minute the shock wave knocked down all the trees for miles around. Millions of trees snapped at their bases and fell to the ground. It looked as though a giant hand had scattered toothpicks on the slopes.

Thunder rumbled above the mountain. Lightning flashed. The lightning struck the ground and started many fires. Soon thousands of acres of the forest blazed.

Hot ash, rock, and dirt from Mount St. Helens fill the sky.

Hot gases from the explosion swept over fields of ice and snow and down the mountainside. The extreme heat of the gases caused snow and ice to melt instantly. This water mixed with dirt from the landslide, falling ash, and the hot gases to form a wall of boiling mud. The mud steamed and roared down the mountain and into the Toutle River. There was so much mud that it pushed the water over the river banks.

Trees fell like giant toothpicks on the slopes of the volcano.

The first of four mudflows pushed a wall of roaring water that swept away bridges on the Toutle River.

Soon the river grew to many times its normal size. The flood waters swept away bridges, uprooted trees, and killed animals. Afterwards, the original narrow riverbed no longer existed. Instead, many tiny streams cut through a newly formed landscape of gray mud.

Spirit Lake two months after the eruption.

A second mudflow surged into Spirit Lake. Half the lake was filled. Mud, rocks, and fallen trees quickly piled up at one end. A dam two hundred feet high and more than a mile wide formed.

Water from the melting fields of snow and ice poured into Spirit Lake. The dam stopped the water from flowing down the mountain. Within minutes the water level had risen one hundred feet behind the dam and continued to rise. There was a danger that the dam would break. If it did, the backed-up water would flood the valley below Spirit Lake. The lives of fifty thousand people were threatened. Over the next few days, however, this danger lessened. The water in Spirit Lake slowly leaked through the mud dam and flowed down the mountain.

This destructive eruption greatly changed the shape of the mountain. Mount St. Helens is no longer 9,677 feet high. One-seventh of its height was blasted away. A new crater was formed where the peak used to be. Spirit Lake has almost disappeared. The outlines of the hills and ridges of the mountain have changed forever.

The earth is not quiet and stable. Quickly or slowly, it is changing all the time. Volcanoes are just one of the forces that build up or tear down mountain chains. The eruption of Mount St. Helens is one tiny event in the series of changes that have been taking place on earth for billions of years.

2   Run for Your Lives

Most of the people who lived on the slopes, cut logs in the forests, and hiked along the trails of Mount St. Helens did not realize that the mountain would become an active volcano. After all, it had been quiet for 123 years. But many scientists were not surprised when the volcano came to life. In 1975, they had predicted that Mount St. Helens would erupt sometime during the next 25 years.

In March 1980, the warning signs began when a series of small earthquakes shook the mountain. Scientists set up several look-out posts and watched the mountain day and night. Even though they were fairly certain that it was getting ready to erupt, they could not predict when the eruption would occur. It could be within a week, or it might not happen for several years.

The answer came on March 27, 1980. Suddenly, smoke blasted out the top of Mount St. Helens and mushroomed into the sky. Near the top of the mountain appeared a huge crater and many large cracks. The volcano had awakened!

Small eruptions continued for more than a week. Each eruption spewed smoke, ash, and gas high into the air. Mud

Mount St. Helens on April 10, 1980, about five weeks before the May 18 eruption.

slides rolled down the upper slopes of the mountain. A second crater formed. Gradually the two craters became larger and joined into one huge one.

The danger signals did not go away. Government officials watched the mountain closely. They feared a more violent eruption that could hurt or kill anyone caught on the slopes of the volcano. The officials declared the area within fifteen miles of the peak a danger zone and asked all the people inside this zone to leave. People living on the mountain packed up their belongings and left. All the roads leading up the mountain were closed.

In early April, scientists became excited by a new series of earthquakes. These were harmonic tremors—long, steady, mild movements in the earth. Harmonic tremors differ from the sharper bursts of other earthquakes. They occur when melted rock moves beneath the earth's surface. Scientists began to think that this melted rock was going to erupt from Mount St. Helens.

A fairly calm period followed the harmonic tremors. From time to time ash and steam from small eruptions shot into the air. No earthquakes, however, shook the mountain. Scientists wondered whether the volcano was going back to sleep.

Then, in late April, people became alarmed again. The north side of the mountain started to bulge. The mountain was swelling from the pressure of the melted rock moving toward the surface. Scientists warned that the volcano could erupt with great force. If it did, glowing hot mud and ash could reach as far down the mountain as Spirit Lake, four thousand feet below the summit.

Mount St. Helens was still not deserted. Even though the chances of a dangerous eruption seemed to increase daily, a

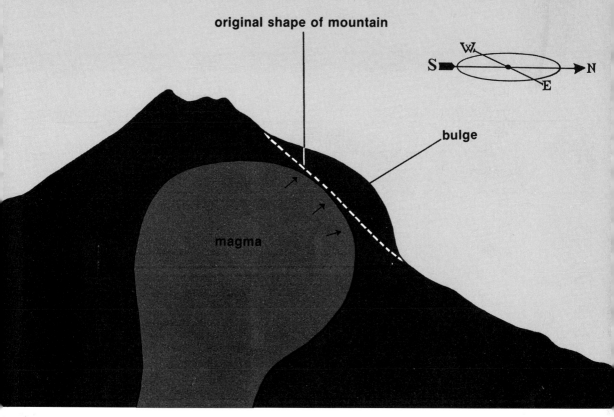

Magma inside Mount St. Helens pressed against the north slope to form a bulge.

team of scientists continued to watch the volcano. Every day one or more of the team climbed the slopes to gather information. All the scientists knew that the erupting mountain could kill them. Yet they were willing to risk their lives to study a volcano in action. David Johnston spoke for all the scientists when he compared Mount St. Helens to "a dynamite keg with the fuse lit."

By now, Mount St. Helens had become a tourist attraction. Sightseers came from far and near. Everyone—fathers, grandmothers, children—wanted to see an active volcano. Again and again, the police tried to keep residents, sightseers, and loggers

Police set up roadblocks to keep sightseers away from the volcano.

away. But some people did not really believe the volcano would erupt. They did not take these warnings seriously.

Harry Truman was determined to stay. The eighty-three-year-old man ran a lodge on Spirit Lake, at the base of the mountain. He had lived there for more than fifty years. Truman told reporters, "No one knows more about this mountain than Harry, and it don't dare blow up on him." Despite many attempts to convince Harry to leave his home, he refused.

Some property owners became angry when they were blocked from their homes and cabins on the mountain. They worried more about thieves breaking into their homes than about the volcano destroying them. On Saturday, May 17, the state police took a group of these people to their cabins near

Near Mount St. Helens, a scientist gathers samples for testing.

Spirit Lake. The owners loaded their valuables into trucks and drove down the mountain. They got out just in time.

The next day, Mount St. Helens stopped being entertainment and became a gruesome nightmare. The bulging north face of the mountain blew off. Most of the people on or near the mountain were killed.

David Johnston was only five miles from the top of Mount St. Helens when it exploded. His excited cry crackled over the radio waves: "Vancouver! Vancouver! This is it!" Then there was silence. Scientists in Vancouver, Washington, waited anxiously. But they never heard from David again. He died doing the work he loved most. Harry Truman was also killed that day, along with his sixteen cats.

The mountain did not observe the official boundary and roadblocks when it erupted. Even people in areas thought to be safe found themselves in grave danger.

Thirty miles from the top of Mount St. Helens, six young adults had pitched their tents in a deserted campground. On the morning of the eruption, the forest was unusually quiet. Only the sounds of the campers broke the stillness. Bruce Nelson, Sue Ruff, and Terry Crall were cooking breakfast. Suddenly they felt a burning wind on their faces. They looked up. A monstrous yellow and black cloud was about to close in on them. Terry sped to the tent to alert Karen Varner. Bruce and Sue clung to each other in terror. Trees fell all around them. Poisonous gases choked them. Stones, hot ash, and clumps of mud rained down. The stones cut and bruised them. The ash and mud made them gag.

Frantically, Bruce and Sue dug themselves out. The ash burned their hands. They called out to their friends. No answer came from Karen and Terry. Logs and ash covered Karen's tent.

Bruce and Sue heard feeble cries from Brian Thomas and Dan Balch, the other two members of the group. They found Brian under a log. He seemed dazed and his hip was broken. He could only walk with help. Dan was seriously hurt. Severe burns from the hot ash covered his arms, hands, and legs. He was in shock and could not walk at all.

An old mine shack provided shelter and safety for Dan and Brian while Sue and Bruce went for help. For fifteen miles the two young people waded through deep ash and climbed over fallen trees as they searched for a way out of their waking nightmare. They could feel the heat of the ash through their shoes. After a time they met a sixty-year-old man. The three survivors sang songs to cheer themselves up as they trudged away from the mountain.

Following tracks in the ash, rescuers in helicopters spotted the trio and carried them to safety. Soon another rescue team brought out Brian and Dan. Karen and Terry were found dead.

A footprint in the volcanic ash.

A helicopter lands on the ash near Mount St. Helens shortly after the May 18 eruption.

Roald Reiten and Venus Dergen were camping near the Toutle River about twenty-three miles below Spirit Lake. On the morning of May 18, they slept late. While they slept, the volcano erupted. Thousands of trees fell into the river and headed their way. A loud rumbling awakened the sleeping campers. They stumbled out of the tent. Logs jammed the river, and the water was rising rapidly. Roald and Venus raced to the car. They were too late. Flood waters already covered the road. As Roald and Venus looked for another way out, a wall of mud crashed through the forest and surged toward them. They scrambled onto the roof of the car, but it was useless. The mud pushed the car into the river. They found themselves thrown into the hot, muddy water. Logs, clumps of mud, and pieces of train trestle swirled around them. Roald pulled himself up onto a log. The logs trapped Venus in the water. She went under several times. Again and again Roald grabbed for her. Suddenly, a space opened between the logs. Roald grabbed once more. This time he caught hold of Venus! He pulled her up onto the log with him.

The river carried Roald and Venus downstream. Several people spotted them and helped them out of the river.

Not everyone near the mountain that day had to be rescued. Vern Hodgson, like many others, brought his camera when he came to view Mount St. Helens. On the morning of May 18, Vern set his camera up to take pictures of the snow-capped peak fifteen miles to the southwest. Suddenly, the distant mountain-side began to slide. Smoke poured out into the sky. Vern snapped one picture after another until he used up his film. Then he jumped into his van and drove away. He had not gone far before ash started to fall.

Vern covered his mouth and nose with a towel so that he could breath. Every few minutes he stopped and got out of the van to clean the ash off the windshield. After hours of slow driving, he finally reached his home. Vern had taken a perfect series of photographs of the eruption.

Many other people experienced the eruption of Mount St. Helens on May 18, 1980. At least forty-nine of them are dead or missing. The bodies of many of the victims have not been found and may be buried beneath the ash forever. Those who lived have their own stories to tell of escape or rescue. For years to come, friends and relatives will be hearing stories of "how I survived the great volcanic eruption of 1980."

3 A Mountain of Mud

Whenever rain falls or snow melts on Mount St. Helens, the water trickles into tiny streams. As the streams flow down the mountain, they join with other tiny streams and become larger. The water cascades noisily down the slopes. It tumbles over waterfalls and crisscrosses Mount St. Helens. Before the eruption, the waters teemed with fish.

On the lower slopes of the mountain, the larger streams turn into fast-moving rivers that cut paths through deep forests. Lumberjacks harvest trees on these slopes and float the logs down the rivers to sawmills.

The Toutle River begins on Mount St. Helens and empties into the Cowlitz. This river flows southward into the slow-moving Columbia. In time the water flowing through the Columbia River reaches the Pacific Ocean. The Columbia is so deep and so wide that huge ocean-going ships are able to travel upstream to its inland harbors. In both Oregon and Washington, many businesses use the river to ship needed supplies in and finished products out. The people working in these businesses depend on the Columbia and the other rivers for their jobs.

Water cascades down the mountain at the start of its long journey to the ocean.

The explosion of Mount St. Helens caused great changes in the rivers that drain the mountain. Within an hour of the eruption, the first of four mudflows surged down the Toutle River at speeds of up to thirty-five miles per hour. The boiling mud pushed ahead of it a wall of water that flooded the river. The raging flood waters smashed bridges, killed animals, and washed away homes. They destroyed a logging camp and slammed huge trucks on end as if they were toys. The floods even knocked a freight train off its tracks.

Raging floodwaters knocked a freight train off its tracks.

The Toutle River after the floodwaters and mudflows had swept over its banks.

When Mount St. Helens erupted, thousands of logs, placed in the river by lumberjacks, were floating downstream. The floods uprooted many trees and knocked them into the water. As the mudflows surged down the river, all these logs and fallen trees smashed into each other and piled up together. For twenty miles the river became wall-to-wall trees. In fact, logs were packed so tightly in some places that people could walk across the river.

The floods washed thousands of trees and parts of broken bridges and homes into the Columbia River. Huge amounts of mud from Mount St. Helens settled to the bottom of the river. So much mud and other material filled up the Columbia that no large ships could pass through. Thirty-one ocean-going ships suddenly became trapped in inland harbors. Shipping halted along the Columbia River.

The destructive mudflows almost buried this now-abandoned mailbox.

Each day that the ships sat idle, people could not work, and businesses could not meet their orders. Someone had to clear an emergency shipping lane through the mud as quickly as possible. Then ships could begin moving on the river again. The U.S. Army Corps of Engineers came to the rescue. Working day and night, the engineers used their dredges to remove mud from the river bottom.

Within one week, ships began to move slowly and carefully up and down the river. But that was only the beginning of the job for the Army Corps of Engineers. It would take months to restore the shipping lane to its normal size. Now, at least, the ships were moving.

Shipping was not the only thing that was stopped by the

U.S. Army Corps of Engineers dredges remove mud from the bottom of the Columbia River.

eruption of Mount St. Helens. In Longview, Washington, mud from the volcano buried the pipe that carries water from the Cowlitz River to the town. Mud also clogged the pumps that bring water to the water treatment plant. Since the plant could not function, the people of Longview had no water. They could not bathe or flush toilets. There was no water to drink. Firefighters feared disaster. They had no way to put out fires.

Officials decided to pump in water from nearby Kelso. There was just enough water for both towns. Even though the people of the two towns had to limit their water use, the real crisis was over.

The mudflows from Mount St. Helens endangered the

animals that lived in the Toutle River. Each time boiling mud gushed through the river, the water became hotter. The high temperatures instantly killed millions of fish. Many fish that tried to escape the heat by jumping out of the water died on the dry river banks. Farther downstream where the water was not quite as hot, their gills became clogged with ash as they breathed. Many of these fish died from lack of oxygen. Tiny glass bits in the ash cut the gills of other fish and caused them to become sick and die.

Many of the fish killed in the streams and rivers of Mount St. Helens were salmon. Normally, millions of tiny salmon hatch from eggs in the early spring. They feed and grow in the clear mountain water. When the salmon are about a year old, they swim downstream, all the way to the ocean. For several years the salmon live in the ocean. They eat greedily and grow rapidly. When the fish are fully grown, they get an urge to return to their home streams.

The adult salmon retrace their earlier journey. This time, however, they must swim upstream. After traveling for several months, the salmon reach the streams where they were hatched. Here the salmon lay their eggs and die. The following spring the eggs hatch, and the cycle begins again. This cycle was unbroken for centuries. The eruption of Mount St. Helens may disturb it in the future.

Materials dissolved in water give each river a distinct odor that the fish recognize. The salmon find their way home by sensing the odor of the water. The water in the rivers affected by the volcano is now filled with different materials. It contains ash from inside the volcano, and mud and stones from high up on the mountain. Even if most of this material is carried away, the odor of the water will probably be changed. What will

The mudflows widened the banks of many of the rivers and streams on the slopes of Mount St. Helens.

happen when the salmon that are now in the ocean try to return home? Will the rivers and streams smell the same? Scientists can only guess, but they fear that many salmon will not be able to find their home streams. If that happens, the salmon will not lay their eggs.

There is another concern about these fish. Salmon lay their eggs on gravel beds. Fine mud from the volcano has now settled to the bottom of the streams and covered the gravel. Even if the fish do find their way home, they may not lay any eggs.

The end of the mudflows and ashfall did not mark the end of the danger from the volcano. A few days after the eruption, a mudflow had formed a new dam at Spirit Lake. The water level

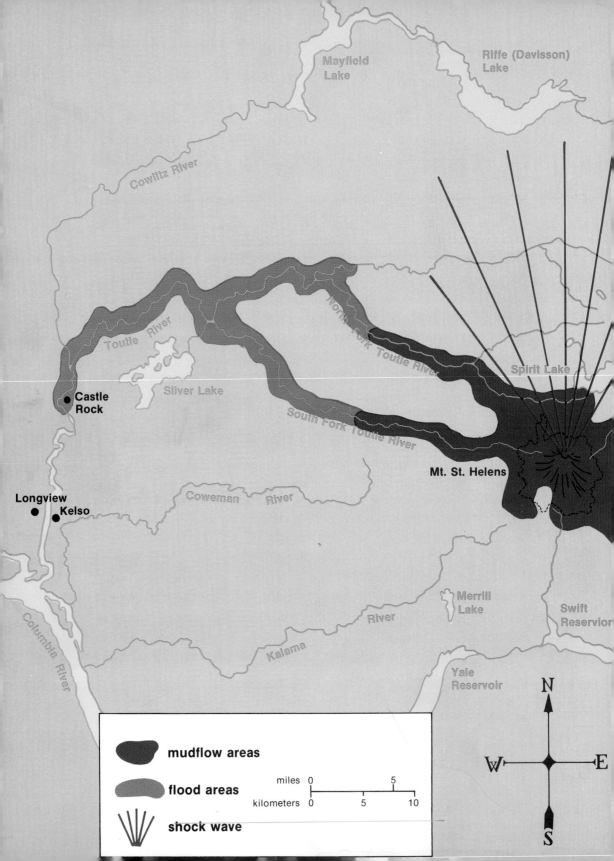

Mayfield Lake

Riffe (Davisson) Lake

Cowlitz River

Toutle River

North Fork Toutle River

Spirit Lake

Castle Rock

Silver Lake

South Fork Toutle River

Longview

Kelso

Coweman River

Mt. St. Helens

Merrill Lake

Swift Reservoir

River

Columbia River

Kalama

Yale Reservoir

N

W E

S

mudflow areas

flood areas

miles 0   5

kilometers 0   5   10

shock wave

13550

of the lake had risen two hundred feet. Earthquakes had been very common before the eruption. An earthquake now could easily loosen the dam and send another, even larger, wall of water down the Toutle River.

Mud from the first floods had settled to the bottom of the river and raised the riverbed. If more water came, it could easily spread farther over the river banks than it had in the first floods. It could destroy even more homes and land.

All along the rivers where flood waters from the mudflows had just raged, people were told to leave their homes. As far away as Kelso and Longview, people living near the river took their belongings and moved to high ground. They slept in schools and churches.

Many people did not know what to think. They could no longer see Spirit Lake, which was hidden behind steam and clouds of ash from the volcano. Scientists could not see what was happening, either. For days, people listened to flash flood warnings on the radio. They moved out of their homes, bought flood insurance, and waited.

Finally, on May 22, scientists could see the lake again. Water was seeping slowly out through small cracks in the dam. The level of the lake had fallen one hundred fifty feet below the top of the dam.

By May 26, the danger that the dam might burst was almost completely gone. The water level had dropped another fifty feet. People thankfully returned to their homes.

Some of the changes in the rivers lasted for only a few weeks or months. Other changes are more long-lived. The course of the Toutle River itself has been altered. Places that were once dry land are now at the bottom of the river. Here, as everywhere, the story of the volcanoes is also the story of the changing land.

This map shows the direction of the blast wave from the eruption and the mudflow and flood areas around Mount St. Helens.

4 The Blizzard of Ash

When Mount St. Helens erupted, about one cubic mile of solid mountain exploded into the atmosphere. Boulders and large rocks fell back to earth at once. Smaller rocks and stones traveled short distances before dropping to the ground. But the tiny ash particles from inside the volcano stayed suspended in the air. Strong winds carried them rapidly toward the northeast. Skies darkened as ash fell on eastern Washington and parts of Montana and Idaho. Street lights came on automatically in midday. Visibility was near zero.

Not all the ash fell to earth. Fast-moving winds high in the atmosphere carried some of it around the world. Some weather reporters predicted a drop in global temperatures if the ash blocked enough of the sun's rays.

Although the falling ash looked like a blizzard of snow, it was not at all like a winter storm. Snowflakes are water crystals. Ash bits are tiny glasslike particles. Snow is white and soft. Ash is gray and gritty. Snow melts. Ash does not. People know what to expect when snow falls. Falling ash was new and unfamiliar.

Ash rises from Mount St. Helens high into the sky.

A layer of ash coated roads and cars. When the wind gusted, motorists could barely see the highway ahead. Ash clogged the air filters of cars and caused the engines to stall. There were many small accidents as automobiles skidded on streets slick from ash. Police closed roads. Hundreds of travelers were stranded at schools, churches, and restaurants. Some did not get home for days.

Most buses, trains, and airplanes did not move. Businesses, schools, and libraries were closed. Of the few cars on the road, most were patrol cars. Police officers had to be on duty to take care of people who needed help. By the end of the week, ash had ruined sixty of Washington's state police cars. Finally, an ingenious person put together a complex system of air filters with long hoses that wound halfway around the cars. At first glance you might have thought the patrol cars were spaceships from other worlds. At least this way the cars could be used.

Since most people had never encountered volcanic ash, they had a lot of questions. Is the ash dangerous? Will it burn your skin? How do you clean it up?

Rumors flew. Conflicting information about the ash confused people. Some reports cautioned that it was dangerous. Others said that it was harmless. Some reports claimed that breathing through a wet cloth was the best thing to do. Others said that it was the worst. Some reports warned that ash mixed with water contained sulfuric acid and would burn your skin. Others said that was nonsense.

Everyone agreed that the ash was a nuisance. The best thing to do was to stay indoors until it had stopped falling. As the days passed, people learned that the ash was not deadly or very acidic.

Volcanic ash gives people dry and itchy throats and noses. To

A Washington state police car uses wraparound air filters to deal with the ash.

breathe more easily in ash-filled air, you need a mask to filter out the fine particles. At first police and fire fighters wore gas masks that made them look like Halloween monsters. The masks turned out to be of little use, however, since their filters were quickly clogged with ash. The police and fire fighters then switched to surgical masks. These made them look like doctors.

In order to cope with the ash, people became resourceful. They discovered a new use for coffee filters. When rigged up with string and a little tape, a coffee filter turns into a face mask that filters ash out of the air. Other people tied handkerchiefs

over their noses and mouths, outlaw-style. Enterprising young people stood on street corners and sold ready-made masks for fifty cents each. Everyone on the streets had their faces covered. There was one problem, however, that no one had foreseen. Bank tellers feared stickups from every customer that walked through the door!

Throughout the Northwest, people packed ash into envelopes and sent it to friends and relatives across the country. Many of the envelopes burst open as they passed through postal machinery. The gritty ash caused the machines to break down. As a result, mail service slowed and even stopped in some towns. Post office officials urged the public to mail ash only in plastic bags that would not break.

Mount St. Helens's ash seemed to be everywhere and in everything. It was on roofs and sidewalks, trees and lawns, streets and cars. It got in people's clothes, on cats' fur, and in goldfish bowls. Sometimes it even found its way into cookie jars!

Some people tried to shovel the ash off their roofs and sidewalks. The wind, however, just blew if back again. Those who hosed down their gardens found that the powdery ash turned to a gray slurry that was even harder to remove. Washing cars didn't do much good, either. The swirling ash from the road quickly coated them again.

Nowhere did repair manuals explain what to do about volcanic ash in washing machines. Some people learned, to their dismay, that laundry soap, water, and ash combined to form a gray sludge that hopelessly clogged the machine. Others discovered, to their relief, that laundry detergent did not create

Young people in Yakima, Washington, wear protective face masks as they sweep up Mount St. Helens ash.

U.S. Army helicopters helped in the massive campaign to clean up the ash.

this problem. Slowly, by trial and error, people learned how to deal with the strange material all around them.

Thousands of acres of fruit trees were blanketed by the gray ash. Fruit growers feared the loss of all their apples, cherries, pears, and peaches. Some orchard owners sprayed their trees with water or air to remove the ash. Others hired helicopter pilots to fly three or four feet above the treetops. The wind from the spinning blades blew the ash off the leaves and fruit.

Crime came almost to a standstill. Perhaps potential

criminals learned a lesson from one unlucky man. This would-be burglar tried unsuccessfully to break into a store through a window. The store owner discovered the damage and called the police to the scene. A set of unbroken footprints led away from the window. The police followed them to a mobile home, where the tracks ended at the door. An officer checked the boots of the man inside. The boots matched the tracks exactly. The man was arrested.

Despite all the problems created by the ash, most people kept their sense of humor. One joker suggested that the *W* in Washington be dropped in order to change the name of the state to "Ashington." A sign at the ash-covered airport in Spokane said, "REJOICE, IT IS ASH WEDNESDAY." The owner of an auto body shop in Yakima put up a sign that proclaimed, "DON'T BE FOOLED BY SUBSTITUTES—ST. HELENS DUST 50¢ A GALLON."

Road crews removed thousands of truckloads of ash from the streets with snowplows and heavy earth-moving equipment. Only with time, however, can the cities, towns, and farms be completely cleaned up. Rain must do the final job. Here, as in all the volcanic regions of the world, the rains slowly pound the gray grit into the ground. As the years pass, the ash enriches the soil.

5   The Science of Volcanoes

Once upon a time, according to an old Indian legend, there lived a powerful chief with his two sons. Both sons fell in love with the same beautiful Indian princess. Each one wanted her for himself so much that he fought against his brother for her love. The princess was flattered by the attention and felt very important. She did not want to choose between the brothers. They waged bigger and bigger battles as they attempted to win the princess's affection.

Finally, the Great Spirit became angry with the brothers for fighting all the time. He became angry with the princess for not making a choice. In his anger, he covered each of the three young Indians with stone and turned them into separate mountains. The princess is in Mount St. Helens. Most of the time she sleeps quietly there. But every hundred years or so, something disturbs her rest. Then she awakens and blows the top off the mountain.

American Indians are not the only people who have used legends to explain natural events such as volcanic eruptions. Throughout history people have told stories and myths to

A volcano erupts in the Hawaii Volcanoes National Park.

explain things they did not understand. The word *volcano* comes from an ancient Roman myth. The Romans believed in Vulcan, the god of fire. Vulcan was a powerful blacksmith who lived deep inside volcanoes. Whenever he worked, the mountains rumbled loudly, and sparks from his forges flew out the top.

Other groups of people believed that volcanoes were inhabited by gods. Some of these groups offered human sacrifices to the gods. In this way they hoped to keep the gods from getting angry and causing the volcanoes to erupt.

It may still be easier to explain volcanic eruptions with romantic stories of gods and princesses. For centuries, however, some people have wanted to know more. They wanted to know what really causes hot ash and melted rock to explode or pour out of volcanoes. To find out, they began by studying the inside of the earth.

The earth is very hot inside. What do you think would happen if you tried to dig a hole straight to the center of the earth? When you first began to dig, you would not notice any change in temperature. But as you dug deeper and deeper, you would get hotter and hotter. For every sixty feet that you went into the earth, the temperature would rise about 1° F. If you ever made it to the center of the earth, it would be very hot indeed! Some of this heat was created billions of years ago when the earth formed. The rest is given off as a result of physical changes inside the earth.

As you journeyed toward the center of the earth, you would also notice changes in the tunnel around you. You would pass through three distinct layers. For the first thirty miles (or less, if you were under the ocean), you would see hard, familiar rock. This thin layer is called the crust. Then you would travel for

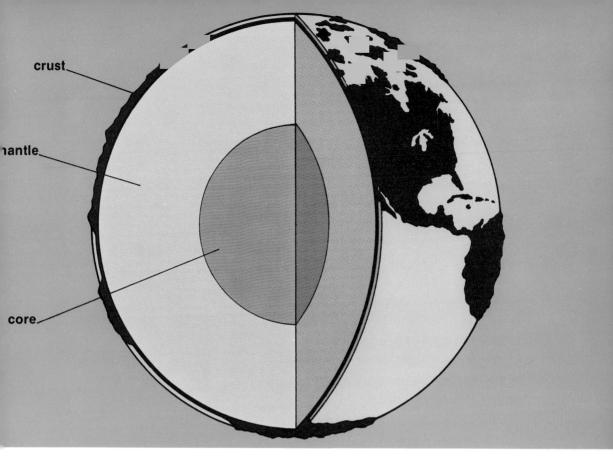

crust

mantle

core

The earth's three layers: the crust, the mantle, and the core.

miles and miles—about eighteen hundred miles—through a layer of very hot rock, called the mantle. During the last twenty-one hundred miles, from the end of the mantle to the center of the earth, you would pass through the earth's liquid core.

The rock in the mantle is different from the rock in the crust. Because mantle rock is very hot, it acts like both a liquid and a solid. Like taffy, it will bend easily if it is moved slowly. If it is hit with a sudden force, however, it will crack. On the earth's surface, rock that is this hot would expand and become liquid. In the mantle, the weight of the crust pushes down on the rock and causes great pressure. Because the hot rock has no room to expand, it stays in solid form.

Sometimes the forces acting on the earth become unbalanced. Then sudden breaks occur. These breaks cause the pressure to change. As the pressure is lowered, earthquakes occur. The hot rock is able to expand and melt, and the melted rock is pushed up to the surface through these breaks.

Such melted rock is called magma. Magma contains water vapor and other gases. It may have a lot of these gases or just a little. The gases are part of magma in the same way that carbon dioxide is part of soda pop. You cannot see or hear the carbon dioxide in an unopened bottle because it stays dissolved in the soda pop. When the bottle is opened, however, you can see bubbles and hear fizzing as the gas slowly escapes.

If you shake a sealed bottle of soda pop, pressure builds up. When the bottle is opened, the gas rushes out with great force. It pushes some of the liquid out of the bottle with it.

Volcanoes act in the same way. The gases in the magma are under great pressure. If the earth's crust develops a weak spot and cracks, an opening may form on the surface. The pressurized gases help push the magma up through the cracks and out the opening. The opening is the volcano. Most of the gases escape from the magma. Once the magma flows out of the volcano, it is called lava.

Scientists group erupting volcanoes as quiet, explosive, or intermediate. Quiet volcanoes make very little noise as they erupt. Their magma flows easily and contains little gas. Small bubbles rise through the liquid, come together to form larger bubbles, and then escape from the magma. The liquid lava flows out quietly. These volcanoes may throw some lava into the air, but they do not explode.

If the lava of a quiet volcano comes out of a long horizontal, or level, crack on the surface, it travels great distances in all

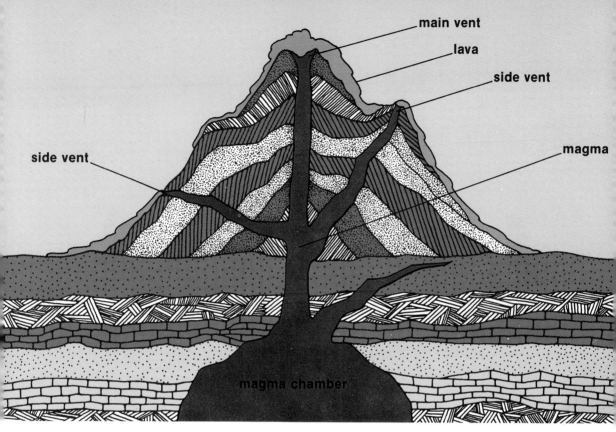

main vent

lava

side vent

side vent

magma

magma chamber

A cross-section of a volcano.

directions. The lava layers from many eruptions pile up on top of each other. Over a long period, the layers may form high plains. The Columbia Plateau in the northwestern United States formed in this way. If the lava flows out of a pipelike hole or vent, it does not travel as far. It slowly builds up a wide, gently-sloping mountain, called a shield volcano. Shield volcanoes that were built up from the ocean floor created the Hawaiian Islands.

Explosive volcanoes erupt with great force. Their magma is very thick and stiff and contains more gas than that of quiet volcanoes. The thick magma rises very slowly, and its gases do not escape easily. As a result, much of the gas is trapped in the

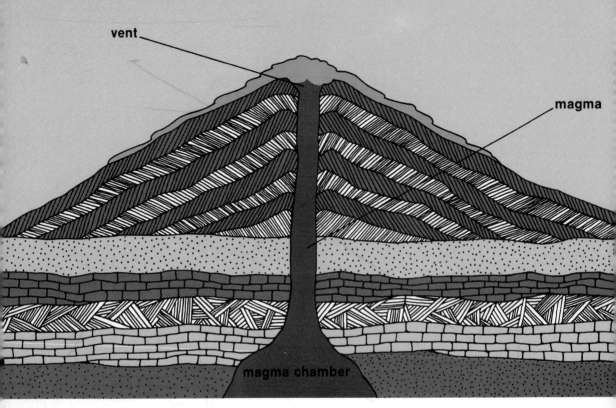

A cross-section of a shield volcano.

magma. The gases build up pressure until they burst out of the volcano. The melted rock does not flow gently away. It explodes into the air. Then it cools quickly and hardens into fine ash, pebble-sized cinders, or large chunks called bombs. The ash, cinders, and bombs pile up around the vent and form a steep volcanic mountain called a cinder cone. Big Craters is a large double cinder cone in Idaho's Craters of the Moon Monument.

After a volcano has erupted, volcanic material may fall back and block the vent. Or thick magma may harden in the vent without ever erupting. In either case, liquid magma can collect beneath the clogged vent. The gases in the magma build up pressure. As the pressure builds, the magma may find another

A cinder cone in Nicaragua, called Cerro Negro, erupted for forty days in 1968.

Mount Rainier was formed by an intermediate volcano.

way out through smaller openings on the side or at the base of the volcano. Such openings have formed on Mount Newberry in Oregon. Mount Newberry is a shield volcano with many small cinder cones on its sides. If the magma under a clogged vent has no other place to go, the gases build up until there is enough force to explode out of the volcano. Violent eruptions such as the one on May 18, 1980, at Mount St. Helens occur in this way.

Sometimes an intermediate volcano erupts quietly. At other times it erupts explosively. As a result, it forms a mountain in which layers of lava alternate with layers of cinders and ash. Mount St. Helens and Mount Rainier were formed by intermediate volcanoes.

There are between four hundred and five hundred active volcanoes on earth. Some erupt often. Others have long periods of quiet between eruptions. Volcanoes that have erupted in modern times but not within recent years are said to be dormant. Mount St. Helens erupted in 1857. It was dormant until the spring of 1980. Now it is active again. Volcanoes that have not erupted within historic times and will probably never erupt again are called extinct.

Some parts of the earth are more likely than others to have erupting volcanoes. In fact, most active volcanoes are found in two great belts. One is called the Mediterranean Belt. It stretches from southern Europe to central Asia. The other belt forms a circle along the edge of the Pacific Ocean. It is called the Ring of Fire. More than 95 percent of the world's earthquakes also occur in these two areas.

The science of plate tectonics explains why most volcanoes and earthquakes are found in the two great belts. The earth's crust is not one unbroken covering. Instead, scientists think the crust is more like the cracked shell of a hard-boiled egg. It is broken into a number of separate sections called plates. Six major plates contain the continents and parts of the ocean floor. Like the pieces of a cracked eggshell, the plates of the earth fit closely together. There are no gaps between them. The Ring of Fire and the Mediterranean Belt mark the edges where crustal plates meet.

Very slowly these plates move over the mantle in different

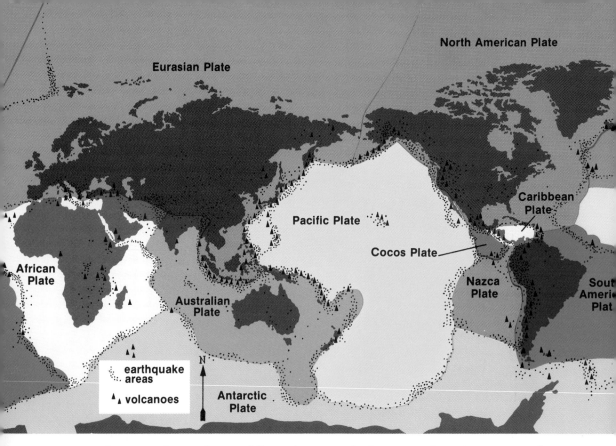

This map shows the world's major crustal plates, earthquake areas, and volcanoes.

directions. As they move, one of three things may happen. The plates may move apart, they may slide past each other, or they may move toward each other.

When plates move apart, magma from the mantle pushes up between them. The melted rock hardens into a giant volcanic mountain range that is split down the middle by a long crack. The mountains are slowly added onto the edges of the two moving plates. New lava comes out of the crack between the mountains. These mountains, called mid-ocean ridges, are found at the bottoms of the oceans. Both volcanoes and earthquakes occur where plates are moving apart.

In other places, the plates slide past each other. The San Andreas Fault in California is the boundary between the North American Plate and the Pacific Plate. The North American Plate carries most of the continent it is named for. The Pacific Plate carries the Pacific Ocean floor and a small slice of western North America. The Pacific Plate moves northward at a rate of 2½ inches a year. Sometimes, though, the two plates stick together, and pressure builds up. Then the plates suddenly lurch past each other. An earthquake results.

When two plates move toward each other, one of them may be slowly bent down and pushed below the other. At the same time, the top plate is being pushed upward. As the two plates are bent, the earth's crust is crumpled, and mountains are formed. The sinking plate heats up and begins to melt into magma. That is what is happening right now near Mount St. Helens. The North American Plate is moving toward the Pacific Plate and forcing the ocean floor under the continent. The ocean floor melts and provides some of the magma for volcanoes. This adds more stress, and earthquakes occur.

The idea of plate tectonics explains past and present volcanoes and earthquakes. It also foretells the future of regions where crustal plates meet. Earthquakes and volcanic eruptions are not going to end in these places. One day Mount St. Helens is likely to blow its top again!

6   Living in the Shadow of Danger

Mount St. Helens erupted with great force and destroyed a large part of the mountain. Even so, this was only a medium-sized eruption compared to those of some other volcanoes. The loss of lives and property was not as great as the losses caused by some of the major volcanic eruptions in the past.

Krakatoa was a small island northwest of Australia. In 1883, a few minor eruptions occurred there. Scientists think these eruptions may have cracked the side of the volcanic cone. Sea water poured in. When it came in contact with the hot magma, the water turned to steam in an instant. The steam expanded. Suddenly the pressure became so great that it blew the island apart.

Almost three thousand miles away in Australia, people heard the explosion. It was one of the most powerful ever recorded. The explosion created giant sea waves nearly one hundred thirty feet high. The giant waves swept over the shores of nearby islands and killed thirty-six thousand people.

Today the volcano is building up a new island. People call it Anak Krakatoa—"child of Krakatoa." Someday this island may explode, just as Krakatoa did.

Another explosive volcano is Mont Pelée on the Caribbean

island of Martinique. Saint-Pierre, a village of thirty-thousand people, lay at the foot of Mont Pelée. For weeks before it erupted in 1902, Mont Pelée belched out warning clouds of ash and black smoke. Suddenly a mixture of gas and boiling mud erupted from the vent of the volcano and killed twenty-three people. The people who lived in Saint-Pierre were worried. The island's governor, however, was not afraid. To convince the people that they had nothing to fear, he moved to Saint-Pierre with his family.

Soon the main vent of Mont Pelée became blocked. The gas and magma inside the volcano could not escape. Pressure built up. The mountain bulged. A huge crack appeared on the side of the mountain facing Saint-Pierre. In a flash gas and magma exploded into the air. A deadly cloud of hot ash and gas surged out of the volcano and sped down the slope. Within one minute almost all the people living in Saint-Pierre died, including the governor and his family.

Only two people survived the eruption. One was a shoemaker who somehow escaped unharmed. The other was a prisoner in the jail. The tiny window in his cell kept out most of the deadly gases. The heat did reach him, however, and he was badly burned. He survived his injuries only to be put in prison in another town.

Italy's Mount Vesuvius is one of the three active volcanoes in Europe. In 63 A.D., it had been dormant for hundreds of years. Suddenly powerful earthquakes rocked the mountain. During the next sixteen years, more earthquakes shook the ground. The Romans did not know that these earthquakes warned of a coming volcanic eruption. They continued to live in the shadow of the volcano.

Mount Vesuvius finally erupted in 79 A.D. Hot ash and

A street and buildings in the ancient Roman city of Pompeii.

cinders rained down on Pompeii and two other cities. Men, women, children, and animals fled down the streets. A few survived. Most fell as they were trying to escape. The ash and other volcanic material quickly buried them and hardened on their bodies. It also hardened on the buildings and trees and completely covered the city.

Seventeen hundred years after the incredible eruption, people finally started to dig through the hardened ash. They found Pompeii and its lifeless inhabitants just as they had been in 79 A.D. The volcano had preserved the city like a museum exhibit. Today people know a lot about the way the Romans lived from studying these ruins.

The remains of a Roman villa in Pompeii.

Vesuvius continues to erupt from time to time, but people still live nearby. Chemicals in the ash make the soil very fertile. Farmers raise excellent crops on the slopes of the volcano.

In many parts of Mexico, just as in Italy, past volcanic activity has greatly enriched the soil. Among the many farmers in this fertile region were once two brothers. The brothers raised good crops and led happy lives. They had one problem, though. There was a mysterious hole in their cornfield. No matter how many times the brothers filled the hole with soil, it always reappeared. They knew the hole had been there for more than fifty years. Yet, they could not understand why it would not stay filled. And no matter how cold the air was, the hole always stayed warm. The brothers could not understand why it was always warm. Often, too, when they worked in the fields, they heard strange noises coming from under the ground near the hole. The brothers could not understand why these sounds were made.

On February 20, 1943, all their questions were answered. The hole in the cornfield widened into a large crack. Loud rumblings came from under the earth. The ground became hot. Then, as one of the brothers watched, the ground around the crack suddenly swelled and rose up eight feet above the field. With a loud hiss, a column of gray ash shot out of the crack and into the sky. The smell of rotten eggs filled the air. A new volcano was born.

The volcano was named Parícutin after a nearby village. It grew rapidly. At the end of the first day, it was 120 feet high. Explosive eruptions continued for months. Five months later, the volcano had built up a cinder cone 1000 feet high and more than half a mile wide.

Ash from the volcano rained down on the houses in the village of Parícutin. Roofs began to cave in under the weight of so much ash. Sadly, the villagers left their homes forever. Later, lava began to flow from the new volcano. Slowly it came toward the deserted village and completely buried it.

The destruction did not end there. Lava continued to flow past the little village. Soon it threatened San Juan, a larger village five miles away. The people of San Juan had to leave their homes, too. Because lava travels slowly, they were able to escape before the melted rock covered their village. Today there is only one reminder that San Juan ever existed. A church steeple pokes up through a hardened lava field.

Parícutin erupted from time to time for nine years before it stopped completely. Scientists think that it will never have another active phase. In just nine years, Parícutin was born, lived, and died.

Parícutin erupting in what was once a Mexican cornfield.

Far more dangerous than Parícutin are the volcanoes of Iceland. Iceland is a snow-covered island nation that has been formed entirely from volcanic materials. Because volcanoes erupt there amid fields of ice and snow, it is sometimes called the Land of Fire and Ice. An eruption occurs somewhere in Iceland about once every six or seven years. Thousands of people make their homes in this dangerous environment. Scattered among the ice fields and volcanoes are many farms and villages.

Throughout Iceland's history volcanic eruptions have played an important part in the life of the Icelandic people. The worst of these eruptions occurred about two hundred years ago. In June 1783, lava began to pour out of a fifteen-mile-long crack called the Laki Fissure. It flowed into a nearby river. Before long the lava filled the river and the surrounding valley to a depth of six hundred feet. Then the melted rock flowed across a flatland and filled a lake. As it moved, the lava destroyed everything in its path—fields, cows, sheep, and entire villages.

One week later, another long crack formed near the first. Again huge amounts of melted rock flowed into the river valley. There was so much of it that it flowed farther than the lava from the first eruption. It cascaded over a steep waterfall and filled the river all the way to the ocean.

A third eruption followed the second. Even more lava entered another river valley and filled that one up, too. Still more fields, animals, and villages were destroyed.

The hot lava quickly melted the ice and snow. Steam from the volcano condensed, or formed water droplets, when it hit the cold air above Iceland. As the steam condensed, heavy rains pelted the island. Since lava blocked many rivers and streams, the water could not drain into the ocean. Widespread floods covered Iceland. Lava poisoned the waters. Deadly gases from the volcano filled the air. Ash fell for miles around. When farm animals ate the ash-covered grass, they became sick and died.

All told, the volcano killed three-fourths of the island's livestock. No fish swam in the poisoned coastal waters. Twenty villages were destroyed. Floods and poisonous gases killed many people. With no livestock or fish to eat, many others soon died of starvation. Altogether, at least ten thousand people died.

A more recent eruption occurred in 1973 on Heimaey, an Icelandic island eight miles from the main island. When people settled Heimaey, they built a town at one end, not far from a dormant volcanic cone. Most of the settlers were fishermen who earned their living from the sea.

Steam rises from the Icelandic island of Heimaey during the 1973 eruption. Cold seawater is being sprayed onto the lava in an attempt to keep it from filling the harbor.

These homes on Heimaey were almost buried by volcanic ash.

One night a new volcano erupted without warning. Hot lava flowed toward the town. Ash and rock rained down on the houses and shops. The people of Heimaey had to leave their island home. One after another, fishing boats pulled up to the docks. The fleeing islanders climbed aboard and were carried to safety. Some people were too old or too sick to go on the boats. Rescuers in helicopters and airplanes flew through thick ash and landed near the moving lava flow in order to save them.

Two hundred people stayed behind to try to save the town and the harbor. By spraying the lava flow with streams of cold water, they were able to slow it down and change its direction slightly. In spite of these efforts, homes caught on fire when hot lava touched them. Shops crashed to the ground under the weight of ash mixed with rainwater. Other buildings were buried under lava and ash. Much of the town was destroyed, and parts of the harbor were filled in.

The word Heimaey means "home isle." People have returned there to dig out their homes or build new ones, simply because it is their home. All over Iceland, people feel the same way. They know they are surrounded by volcanoes. But nowhere else in the world do people speak their language, sing their songs, and share their traditions. And so they stay and live in the shadow of one of nature's most destructive forces.

7   The Cascade Volcanoes

Mount St. Helens is not the only volcano in the western United States. It is just one in a chain of fifteen volcanoes that extends from Canada to northern California. This chain is part of the Cascade Mountain Range, which includes Mount Mazama, Mount Rainier, Mount Newberry, and Lassen Peak. At least twenty more dormant volcanoes are scattered across the western states.

Crater Lake in Oregon rests at the top of what was once a high peak, Mount Mazama. Mount Mazama was formed several million years ago. For a long time, violent eruptions and lava flows alternated with periods of quiet on Mount Mazama. A long quiet period occurred about seven thousand years ago. During this time liquid magma deep within the volcano hardened into solid rock. Gas trapped beneath the rock caused pressure to build up inside the mountain. As more and more gas collected, the pressure mounted.

Finally, the pressure became too great. Cracks formed in the earth's crust, and the gas rushed out. As the gas escaped, one eruption followed another. Ash, cinders, and bombs filled the

Crater Lake in Oregon.

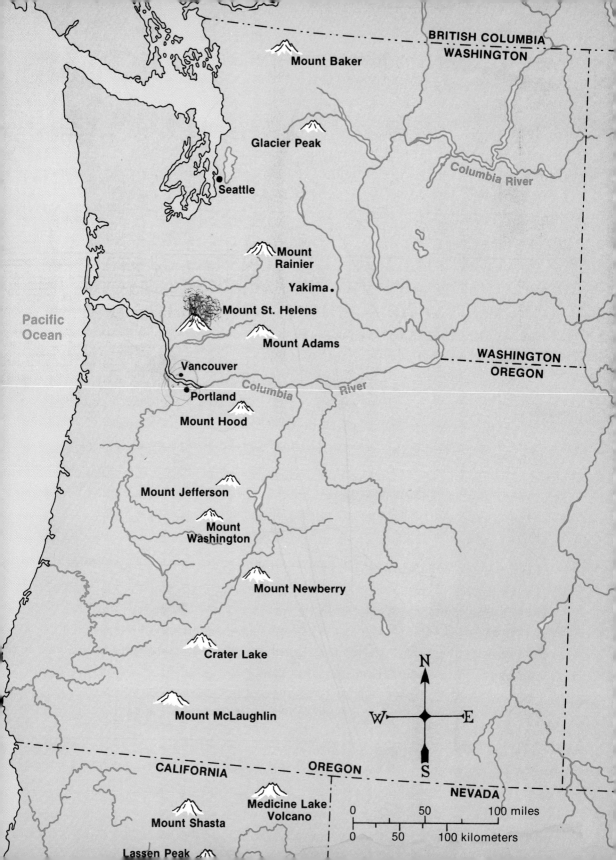

BRITISH COLUMBIA
WASHINGTON

Mount Baker

Glacier Peak

Columbia River

Seattle

Pacific
Ocean

Mount
Rainier

Yakima

Mount St. Helens

Mount Adams

WASHINGTON
OREGON

Vancouver

Portland

Columbia   River

Mount Hood

Mount Jefferson

Mount
Washington

Mount Newberry

Crater Lake

Mount McLaughlin

N

W — E

S

CALIFORNIA   **OREGON**

NEVADA

Medicine Lake
Volcano

Mount Shasta

Lassen Peak

| 0 | 50 | 100 miles |
| 0 | 50 | 100 kilometers |

Most plants cannot survive in this pumice-covered area around Crater Lake.

air. Red-hot ashflows surged down the mountain, and hot gases raced over the slopes.

At last the violent explosions stopped. Then hot gas-filled lava foamed out of Mount Mazama. The bubbling lava cooled quickly and formed pumice, a rock filled with many air holes. So much lava poured out of the volcano that three miles from the summit the pumice is 250 feet deep. Because pumice has so many holes, this thick layer cannot hold water. Rain soaks right through it. Most plants cannot survive such dryness. Today, seven thousand years after the pumice layer formed, this area looks like a desert even though it receives plenty of rain.

This map shows the Cascade volcanoes of the Pacific Northwest.

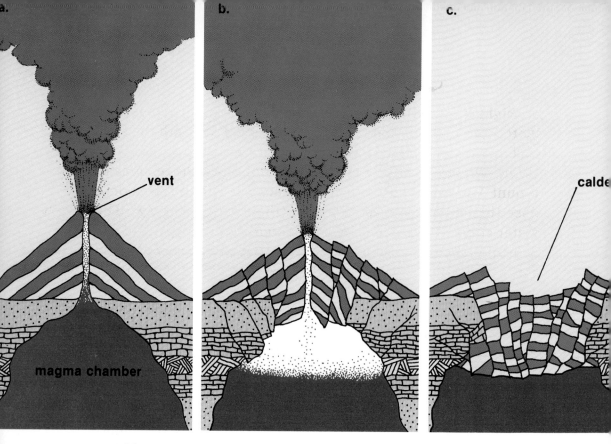

A caldera is created in these stages: (a) a volcano erupts; (b) the magma chamber empties; (c) the mountain collapses, and a caldera forms.

The eruptions of Mount Mazama make those of Mount St. Helens appear small. In fact, so much gas, rock, and magma shot out of Mount Mazama that the main vent and the pool of magma beneath it were totally emptied. The mountain became a hollow shell with nothing to support it. As a result, the entire top of the mountain collapsed into the empty volcano and disappeared.

In the place where Mount Mazama's peak had once been, a huge pit, called a caldera, appeared. Later volcanic activity built up several cinder cones inside the caldera. Then rainwater and melted snow slowly filled the caldera. After many years Crater Lake was formed. One of the cinder cones in the lake looks like an eight-hundred-foot-high island. However, two thousand more feet of this mountain island are hidden beneath the deep blue waters of Crater Lake.

You cannot see Crater Lake as you approach the remains of Mount Mazama. Only when you reach the rim of the caldera does the lake come into view, two thousand feet below. The water stays at the same level. No rivers run into or out of the lake and no springs feed into it. Rain and melted snow fill the caldera at the same rate that the water evaporates into the air.

Crater Lake National Park was established to preserve Crater Lake and the surrounding forests and rock formations. Each year thousands of tourists come to view the ancient volcano. Although it is not active anymore, Mount Mazama is not extinct. It is dormant—no one knows when or if it will erupt again.

The highest of the Cascade volcanoes, Mount Rainier, looks quite large even from Seattle, Washington, fifty-five miles away. People of all ages come to hike, ride horseback, and ski on the trails that crisscross its slopes. As much as eighty feet of snow falls on Mount Rainier each year. Snow and ice cover its summit and upper slopes all year long. Often small snowslides and rockfalls roar down its steep sides.

The mountain's highest point lies between two craters that sometimes belch out steam from deep inside the volcano. In places the hot steam has melted the ice and carved out a network of tunnels and caves. Mountain climbers who reach the peak of Mount Rainier can take shelter from storms and winds inside these caves.

The snow on Mount Rainier may become soggy due to heavy springtime rains or heat from volcanic activity. When the snow becomes waterlogged, it sometimes breaks loose and slides

An ice cave on Mount Rainier.

down the mountain. As it tumbles downhill, the snow picks up rocks, trees, and dirt. Suddenly it becomes a heavy mudflow. Like those that destroyed the Toutle River in 1980, mudflows on Mount Rainier travel quickly. They can bury huge areas with little warning.

In 1947 and again in 1963, fairly small mudflows occurred on Mount Rainier. About five thousand years ago, however, one of the biggest mudflows in the Cascades roared down its slopes. At that time heat and steam inside the volcano caused an entire section of the mountaintop to give way. As the resulting avalanche roared down the mountain, it gathered speed and picked up rocks and trees in its path. A 450-foot wall of mud cascaded into the valley below. Rocks, mud, and trees buried more than one hundred square miles of land. Today, thousands of people live and work on the hills and in the valleys that were once in the path of this mudflow.

Unlike Mount Rainier, Mount Newberry is not near a major city. It does not pose as great a threat to human life. Built mostly from liquid lava, Mount Newberry differs from its neighboring volcanoes in that it is a shield cone. Thousands of years ago, a series of eruptions shot volcanic materials out of the mountain. Afterwards, the top of Mount Newberry collapsed inward. It plugged the main vent and created a large caldera, like the one at Crater Lake. Two small lakes now fill the ends of this caldera.

Mount Newberry has erupted many times since the caldera formed. The most recent eruption happened one thousand years ago. Since the main vent was blocked, the magma from these eruptions followed other pathways out of the volcano. These later eruptions were explosive and blew out ash and rocks. They formed 150 small cinder cones that now stick out of the sides of the mountain.

Mount Newberry is not dead. Heat from inside the mountain is slowly escaping. Gas bubbles rise to the surface of its lakes, and the lake water is warm. At the water's edge, only a few feet into the sand, the temperature is more than 150° F.

Lassen Peak, a dome volcano, marks the southern end of the volcanic chain. At one time, thick, lumpy lava erupted slowly from its main vent. The lava did not spill down the slopes. Instead it hardened into a mushroom-shaped dome above the rim of the vent.

Early white settlers who lived in the shadow of Lassen Peak

Lassen Peak is a dome volcano in northern California.

in northern California thought the volcano would never come to life. But on May 30, 1914, Lassen Peak erupted unexpectedly. During the next three years, it erupted almost four hundred times.

Many of Lassen Peak's outbursts during the first year were mild. Even so, a crater slowly formed at the summit. In the spring of 1915, the eruptions became more violent. Mudflows carrying house-size boulders rushed down the river valleys. Farmers living nearby fled for their lives. A cloud of extremely hot, poisonous gases blasted out of Lassen Peak and knocked down trees for miles around.

Finally, the activity died down. Still, the volcano continued to

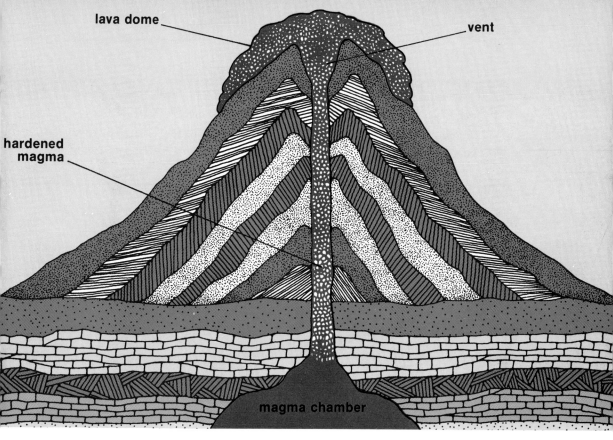

A cross-section of a dome volcano.

erupt from time to time until 1921. Settlers rebuilt their homes, and new people moved into the area. Today visitors climb the mountain and peer into small steaming vents—Lassen Peak's reminder that it is still alive.

The most active volcano in the Cascades is, of course, Mount St. Helens. Most of what can be seen of it has formed during the last one thousand years. Hidden beneath the new peak are the remains of an ancient volcanic cone. Since the time that Columbus sailed to America, Mount St. Helens has erupted about once every hundred years. Each series of eruptions was followed by a period of quiet. The last dormant period began in 1857, after twenty years of activity.

During one eruption, volcanic materials dammed up a valley at the base of Mount St. Helens. Water tumbled down the mountain, flooded the forested valley, and formed Spirit Lake. More than one hundred years later, people in boats could still see the upright trees at the bottom of the lake. But on May 18, 1980, Mount St. Helens again filled the valley and destroyed the crystal clear lake.

Just a week after the huge explosion on May 18, a smaller eruption blasted out of Mount St. Helens. Then a lava dome formed. Later it, too, was blown out of the vent by yet another powerful eruption. The volcano is still not quiet. It continues to throw out hot ash and gas from time to time, and a new lava dome is building.

The danger and excitement of the May 18 eruption were short-lived. Afterwards it took time for people living and working near the volcano to get used to the changes around them. On the slopes of the volcano itself, lumberjacks waded through knee-deep ash to cut up the trees knocked down by the shock wave. More than once these workers had to leave quickly when new clouds of ash erupted from Mount St. Helens.

Along the Toutle River, dredges rebuilt the river channel. People built up the river banks to protect their homes from future floods. A year after the May 18 eruption, the danger was still there. A six-hundred-foot-high wall of volcanic mud and debris blocked the valley through which the Toutle River flowed. If the water trapped behind this huge wall overflows, another flood of mud and water would roar down the valley.

In some areas where the volcanic ash fell, the powdery material washed away quickly when it rained. Life returned to normal. With a few exceptions, crops were not totally destroyed. Since the ash added many important nutrients to the soil, many farmers expect future crops to be better than ever. In fact, some farm areas that were dusted with ash had record harvests of wheat and apples in 1980.

Near Mount St. Helens plant and animal life has begun to reappear. Just two months after the big eruption, small ferns and skunk cabbage were found in sheltered areas on the mountain slopes. In the spring of 1981, fireweed, a pink-flowered bush, added bright touches of color to the dull gray ash and mud. Among the fresh blossoms of spring, honey bees buzzed from flower to flower. In Spirit Lake bacteria and algae have formed the first link in a new food chain. Larger animals such as elk and deer have been seen around watering places not far from the volcano.

If Mount St. Helens follows its past pattern, it will probably continue to erupt for several years. Another dormant period will follow. Then about one hundred years later, the eruptions are likely to begin again.

It is hard to imagine that Mount St. Helens and the other Cascade peaks have not always existed. But millions of years ago, before the dinosaurs lived, these mountains were not here at all. At that time much of what is now the Pacific Northwest was under the ocean. As mud and other materials fell to the ocean floor, the land was slowly built up. Then, much later, rocks in this section of the earth's crust folded over one another, were lifted upward, and formed mountains. As time passed, the action of water and wind slowly wore down these first Cascade mountains. Finally, only rolling hills remained.

Millions of years later, there was a great period of volcanic activity in the Cascades. Lava poured out of long cracks in the ground. So much lava flowed from the earth that it spread for miles and buried some of the older Cascade mountains.

This diagram shows the stages in mountain building. Note the periods of crustal folding and uplift which are reflected in the Cascade Mountains today.

Another period of crustal folding and uplift followed the lava flow. At this time smaller, nonvolcanic mountains were raised to their present heights of four thousand to eight thousand feet. This period, however, was not the end of the mountain building. Since then more volcanic eruptions have built up the higher Cascade peaks. Snow-capped volcanic cones now tower above the folded mountains of the lower Cascades. Their majestic beauty masks their deadliness.

In recent years two other volcanoes in the Cascades have

In the distance Mount Hood rises over Oregon's Willamette Valley.

shown signs of minor activity. These are Mount Baker near the Canadian border, and Mount Hood near Portland, Oregon. For ten thousand years Mount Baker was fairly quiet. Then, in 1975, it erupted mildly. Mount Hood has been quiet for about two thousand years, aside from a small eruption in 1865. In the summer of 1980, however, harmonic tremors were recorded on Mount Hood. These tremors often occur just before an eruption, as they did on Mount St. Helens.

Scientists are watching both Mount Hood and Mount Baker.

Either of these two volcanoes may become active. If they do, scientists hope to warn the public ahead of time about any major eruptions.

Uplift, volcanic activity, and erosion are the forces of nature that change land. Today these forces are still at work in the Cascades. All the Cascade volcanoes have the potential to erupt. Some scientists think that the entire Cascade region is entering a period of increased activity. Not even scientists, however, can be sure of which volcanoes will remain dormant and which ones will become active.

The eruption of Mount St. Helens made headlines all over the United States. For the first time, millions of Americans were made aware of the incredible destructive power of volcanoes. Perhaps the lessons learned from Mount St. Helens will help save lives the next time one of the high Cascade peaks blows its top.

Glossary

active volcanoes—volcanoes that have erupted in recent years

ash—melted volcanic rock that cooled and formed sand-sized pieces when it hit the air

bombs—melted volcanic rock that cooled and formed very large pieces of rock when it hit the air

caldera—a huge pit on top of a volcano formed by the collapse of the cone

Cascade Mountain Range—a mountain range extending along the Pacific Coast from Canada to northern California; it includes Mount St. Helens and fourteen other volcanoes

cinders—melted volcanic rock that cooled and formed pieces the size of pebbles when it hit the air

cinder cones—volcanoes that form when ash, cinders, and bombs pile up around the vent

core—used here to describe the innermost layer of the earth

crater—the bowl-shaped opening of a volcano where volcanic materials come out

crust—used here to describe the outer layer of the earth

dome volcano—a volcano in which the vent has been covered by a mushroom-shaped cap made of hardened lava

dormant volcanoes—volcanoes that have erupted in modern times but not in recent years

dredge—a boat that is equipped for scooping out mud, sand, and other materials from a river bottom

eruption—the sudden release of lava or other volcanic materials from the vent of a volcano

explosive volcanoes—volcanoes that have violent eruptions; their magma cools into ash, cinders, and bombs

extinct volcanoes—volcanoes that have not erupted within historic times and most likely will not erupt again

harmonic tremors—long, steady earthquakes caused by the movement of melted rock under the earth's surface

intermediate volcanoes—volcanoes that erupt quietly at some times and explosively at other times

lava—melted rock that flows out of a quiet or an intermediate volcano

magma—melted rock below the surface of the earth

mantle—used here to describe the inner layer of the earth; the mantle is located between the crust and the core

mudflow—a huge amount of water mixed with dirt and volcanic materials that moves rapidly down a volcano's slopes

plate tectonics—a scientific theory that explains why volcanoes, earthquakes, and mountains are found in certain areas of the world

plates—used here to describe the pieces of the earth's crust; plates fit closely together and move slowly

pressure—the action of one force against another

pumice—a rock filled with many air holes that formed when bubbling lava cooled quickly

quiet volcanoes—volcanoes that erupt with little noise and produce liquid lava

Ring of Fire—a belt along the edge of the Pacific Ocean where volcanoes and earthquakes often occur

salmon—a type of fish that lays its eggs in freshwater streams and lives most of its life in the ocean

shield volcanoes—gently-sloping volcanic mountains built up from eruptions of lava

uplift—an upward movement in the earth's crust that occurs when two plates slowly fold over each other, lift upward, and form mountains

vent—an opening in a volcano where steam and volcanic materials come out

volcano—a place where magma pushes out through a weak spot in the earth's crust; also, the cone formed by a volcanic eruption

Bibliography

Books

Aylesworth, Thomas. *Geological Disasters: Earthquakes and Volcanoes.* New York: Franklin Watts, 1979. Explains the causes of volcanoes and earthquakes, using the theory of plate tectonics. Describes recent earthquakes.

Bianca, Joseph R., editor. *Mount St. Helens—The Volcano.* Portland, Oregon: The Oregonian Publishing Co., 1980. Provides a photographic account of the eruption of Mount St. Helens.

Branley, Franklin M. *Shakes, Quakes, and Shifts; Earth Tectonics.* New York: Thomas Y. Crowell, Co., 1974. Gives a description of plate tectonics and its effects on the earth.

The *Daily News* and the *Journal-American. Volcano, The Eruption of Mount St. Helens.* Longview, Washington: Longview Publishing Co., 1980. Provides a detailed account of the activity at Mount St. Helens and its effects on people.

Fodor, R.V. *The Earth in Motion.* New York: William Morrow and Co., 1978. Explains the behavior of our restless earth, tracing the development of ideas on this subject.

Koenninger, Tom, editor. *Mount St. Helens, Holocaust, The Diary of Destruction.* Lubbock, Texas: C.F. Boone/Barron Publications, Inc., 1980. Gives an account of the eruption of Mount St. Helens and its effects.

Marcus, Rebecca B. *The First Book of Volcanoes and Earthquakes,* revised edition. New York: Franklin Watts, 1972. Explains how and why volcanoes and earthquakes occur.

Matthews, William H., III. *The Story of the Earth.* Irvington-on-Hudson, New York: Harvey House, Inc., 1968. Describes the characteristics of the earth, how it is made up, and how its form has developed. Includes a chapter on volcanoes.

Vaughan-Jackson, Genevieve. *Mountains of Fire, An Introduction to the Science of Volcanoes.* New York: Hastings House, 1962. Explains the science of volcanoes.

Waller, Leslie. *Mountains.* New York: Grosset and Dunlap, 1969. Tells about mountains, where they are, the forces that shaped them, and their effects on life.

Films

Earth: The Restless Planet. National Geographic Society. Shows the volcanoes of Kilauea and Mount Etna, and the inside of Nyiragong caldera in Zaire. Has accompanying game materials.

Earthquakes and Volcanoes. Educational Media, 14 minutes. Explains the causes of earthquakes and volcanoes.

Magazine Articles

Alpern, David M., et al. "The Convulsion of Mount St. Helens." *Newsweek,* Vol. XCV, No. 22 (June 2, 1980), pp. 22-31. Describes the May 18 eruption and its immediate aftermath.

Decker, Barbara and Robert. "The Eruptions of Mount St. Helens." *Scientific American,* Vol. 244, No. 3 (March 1981), pp. 68-80. Tells the history of Mount St. Helens, including an account of the May 18 eruption.

Findley, Rowe. "The Eruption of Mount St. Helens." *National Geographic,* Vol. 159, No. 1 (January 1981), pp. 3-65. Gives a three-part, firsthand account of what happened at Mount St. Helens, fully illustrated.

"God, I Want to Live." *Time,* Vol. 115, No. 22 (June 2, 1980), pp. 26-35. Describes the May 18 eruption and its immediate aftermath.

Index